Collins

ALL ABOUT
SPACE

Published by Collins
An imprint of HarperCollins*Publishers*
1 Robroyston Gate
Glasgow
G33 1JN

HarperCollins*Publishers*
Macken House,
39/40 Mayor Street Upper,
Dublin 1, D01 C9W8, Ireland

collins.co.uk

First published 2025

© HarperCollins*Publishers* 2025

Collins® is a registered trademark of HarperCollins*Publishers* Ltd.

Text by: Laura Baker
'Ask an expert' contribution by: Tom Kerss

Publisher: Beth Rogers
Project leader: Rachel Allegro
Cover and interior design: James Hunter & Rachel Allegro
Editorial: Tracey Cowell & Louise Robb
Production: Ilaria Rovera

Photo credits
All photos © Shutterstock, except: p.11(t): NASA Photo / Alamy; p.35(Johnson): IanDagnall Computing / Alamy; p.37(b): NASA/public domain; p.38(t): Courtesy NASA/JPL-Caltech; p.45(b): Science Photo Library / Alamy; p.47(b): Science Photo Library / Alamy; p.52(t) and 53(b): Christophe Coat / Alamy; p.54(b): Associated Press / Alamy; p.56(t): Naeblys / Alamy; p.61(bl): Peter Gavin Hall / CC BY-SA 3.0; p.63: IanDagnall Computing / Alamy; p.65(tr): IanDagnall Computing / Alamy; pp.68–69(all photos): Tom Kerss; p.80: Art Directors & TRIP / Alamy; p.81(bl): The Picture Art Collection / Alamy

All rights reserved. No part of this publication may be reproduced, stored in a retrieval system, or transmitted, in any form or by any means, electronic, mechanical, photocopying, recording or otherwise without the prior permission in writing of the publisher and copyright owners.

Without limiting the author's and publisher's exclusive rights, any unauthorised use of this publication to train generative artificial intelligence (AI) technologies is expressly prohibited. HarperCollins also exercise their rights under Article 4(3) of the Digital Single Market Directive 2019/790 and expressly reserve this publication from the text and data mining exception.

The contents of this publication are believed correct at the time of printing. Every care has been taken in the preparation of this book. However, the publisher can accept no responsiblity for errors or omissions, changes in detail given or for any expense or loss thereby caused.

A catalogue record for this book is available from the British Library.

ISBN 9780008737559

Printed by LEGO, Italy.

10 9 8 7 6 5 4 3 2 1

This book is produced from independently certified FSC™ paper to ensure responsible forest management. For more information visit: www.harpercollins.co.uk/green

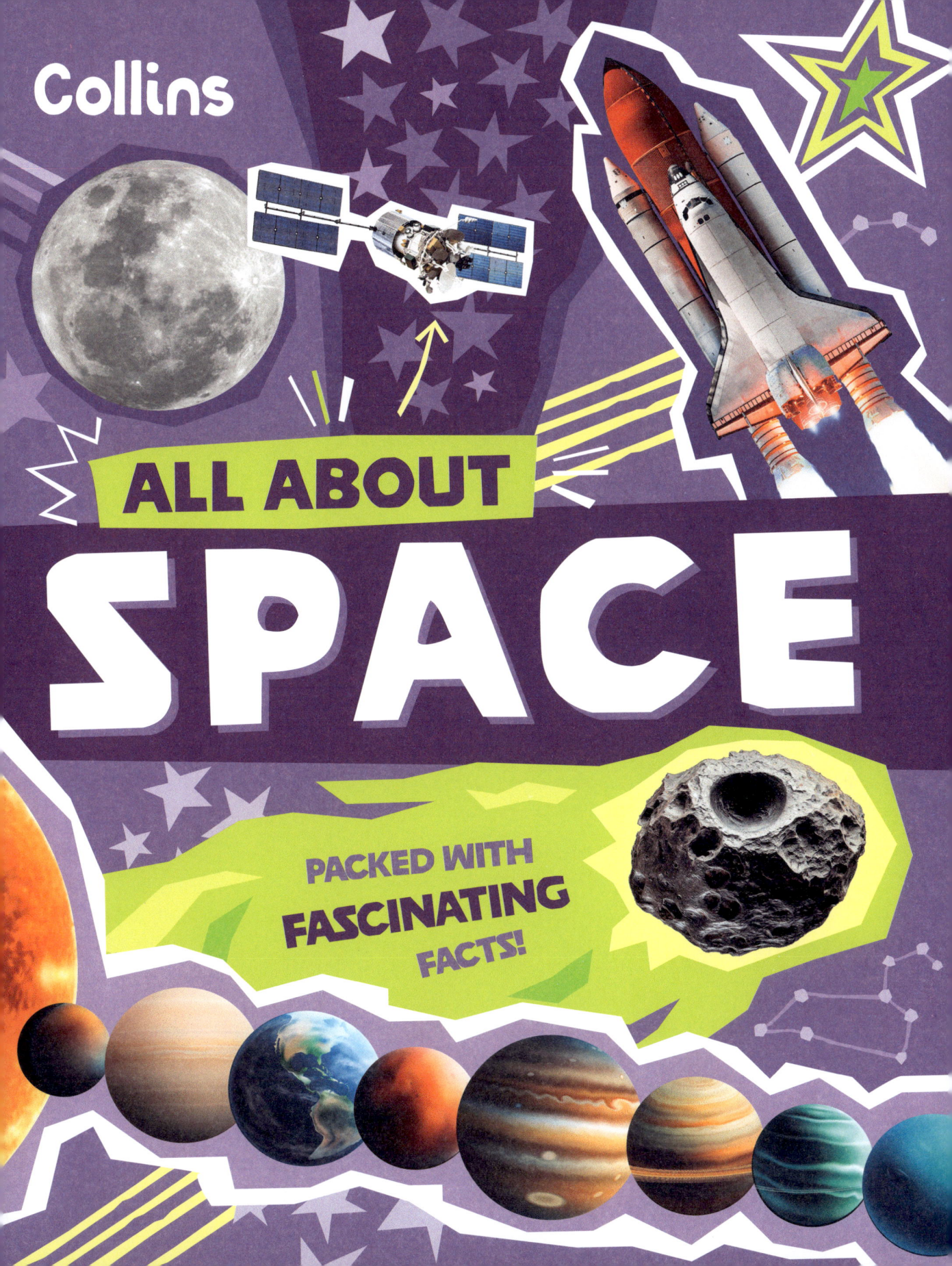

CONTENTS

Welcome to space	8
The universe	10
Galaxies	12
Stars	14
Nebulae	16
Patterns in the stars	18
Name that... Constellation	20
The solar system	22
The Sun	24
Eclipse of the Sun	26
Mercury	28
Venus	30
Earth	32
The Moon	34
Mars	36
The asteroid belt	38
Super stats: Comets and meteor showers	40
Jupiter	42
Saturn	44
Uranus	46
Neptune	48

Name that... Planet 50

Dwarf planets 52

The Kuiper Belt 54

The Oort Cloud 56

Exoplanets 58

Black holes 60

Quiz yourself on...
   Objects in space 62

Space travel 64

Looking into space 66

Ask an expert about...
   The Northern Lights 68

Satellites 70

Rockets 72

The International
   Space Station 74

Rovers 76

Space probes 78

Super stats:
   Space missions 80

Crewed spacecraft 82

The future of
   the universe 84

Quiz yourself on...
   Space exploration 86

Answers 88

Glossary 90

Index 94

Super space

Have you ever thought about what lies beyond the clouds? What's up in the dark night sky? Is there more than just stars? Read on and explore...

WELCOME TO SPACE

If you look up – way up – into the dark night sky, you are looking into space! Although much of it looks empty and black, there are many incredible wonders out there, waiting to be discovered.

Where is space?

Earth is surrounded by a layer of gases, known as the atmosphere. Beyond the atmosphere is what we call space. There is no air or blue sky past this point. The people who study space are called astronomers.

Stars

Most of the objects you see twinkling in the night sky are stars – huge balls of gas that give off light and heat. The Sun is the closest star to Earth.

Galaxies

Galaxies are groups of stars packed together by gravity. They can be home to millions or even billions of stars.

Planets

Some lights in the night sky aren't stars at all, but planets. They are objects that move around the Sun. Unlike stars, planets don't twinkle.

And more

Space holds many other wonders, including orbiting moons, glowing gas clouds, streaking comets, mysterious black holes and more. Discover all about these cosmic curiosities in the pages to come...

Out of this world!

To the skies

For thousands of years, humans could only admire and study space from Earth below. Nowadays, technology such as spacecraft, probes, satellites and rockets allow scientists and astronauts to get up close and into space itself.

FASCINATING FACT

Over 600 people have travelled into space – so far!

THE UNIVERSE

The universe is everything – all matter and all of space together. Within it are billions of galaxies, stars and planets, as well as time, space, energy... and you!

How old?

The universe is about 13.8 billion years old. It all began with the Big Bang.

Major moments

13.8 BILLION YEARS AGO
The Big Bang! All the matter of the universe burst out from one tiny dot of space, and time and space began.

3 MINUTES LATER
Within minutes of the Big Bang, important elements such as helium and hydrogen gases formed.

1 MICROSECOND LATER
In the first fraction of a second, the universe expanded extremely quickly, and the first particles formed.

Light years

The universe is now so vast that it's impossible to measure distances in the units we'd normally use on Earth. Instead, scientists use light years.

Light is extremely fast! It travels through space at 300,000 km per second. One light year is how far light can travel in one year: nearly 10 trillion kilometres. The closest star to us apart from the Sun is 4.25 light years away. If you tried to get there by aeroplane, it would take about 5 million years!

FAMOUS FIGURE: Stephen Hawking

Professor Stephen Hawking (1942–2018) is one of the best-known scientists to discuss the universe. He suggested that because the universe had a beginning, it will also have an end. He also said that the universe has no boundaries, or no edge. Throughout his life, Professor Hawking worked hard to make sure his theories and ideas about the universe were accessible to everybody, not just scientists.

380,000 YEARS LATER
The universe began to cool, a fog cleared and light started to travel freely.

4.6 BILLION YEARS AGO
Earth and the solar system were born.

200 MILLION YEARS LATER
The first stars formed.

400 MILLION YEARS LATER
The stars gathered into galaxies.

NOW
The universe continues to expand!

GALAXIES

Galaxies are groups of stars, planets and clouds of gas and dust. They can contain anywhere from a few thousand stars to trillions of stars!

You are here!

The Milky Way

Our solar system lives in the Milky Way galaxy. This galaxy is shaped like a spiral and is about 100,000 light years across. Earth and our solar system are located between two spiral arms, about halfway from the centre to the outer edge. The galaxy spins in space, and it takes 225–250 million years for Earth to go around just one time.

FASCINATING FACT

The Milky Way gets its name from the way it looks from Earth. If you look up on a clear, dark night, you might be able to see a milky band stretching across the sky.

Nearest neighbour

The closest large galaxy to the Milky Way is the Andromeda Galaxy. It is about 2.5 million light years away. Like the Milky Way, it is a spiral galaxy, but it is more than twice as wide as the Milky Way.

FASCINATING FACT

At the centre of many large galaxies is a supermassive black hole (see p.60).

elliptical galaxy

All shapes and sizes

Galaxies come in many different sizes and shapes. Some, like the Milky Way, are spiral shaped with pinwheel arms. Others can be elliptical, with a round or oval shape. Lenticular galaxies have a disc shape like spiral galaxies, but they don't have any arms. Many galaxies have irregular shapes that give them their name. These include galaxies named after a butterfly, tadpole, spider and hockey stick!

lenticular galaxy

the Tadpole Galaxy

STARS

Stars are huge balls of hot gas in space. Just like living things, a star has its own life cycle – it is born and eventually it dies. This process can take millions or even trillions of years!

Nebula

Stars are born in huge clouds of gas and dust called nebulae. Some of the gas and dust pulls together and becomes an incredibly hot and bright ball that releases energy.

Main sequence

In the longest phase of their lives, stars shine brightly and are called main sequence stars. This stage can last millions or billions of years, depending on the mass of the star.

Red giant

Eventually, fuel within the star begins to run out. The star expands, cools and changes to a red colour.

FASCINATING FACT

Red stars are relatively cool stars. The hottest stars are blue, followed by hot yellow stars, like the Sun.

Planetary nebula

The dying star releases gas and dust. This creates a glowing shell, which looks a bit like a planet from afar, so it is called a planetary nebula.

White dwarf

A white dwarf is the final stage of the star's life. The core of the star remains but cools down over a long period of time, and eventually stops shining.

Supernova

Massive stars become red supergiants and eventually collapse in a huge supernova explosion. Material spreads out across space and forms new nebulae, where new stars will be born... and the cycle begins again!

NEBULAE

These giant clouds of gas and dust can come from dying stars, and they can also be the place where new stars are born.

Star nurseries

Nebulae where new stars are born are known as stellar or star nurseries. Many baby stars might start in the same nebula, before spreading out across the universe.

Helix Nebula

Between the stars

You'll find nebulae in the space between the stars, called interstellar space. The closest nebula to Earth is about 700 light years away. It is called the Helix Nebula.

Planetary nebulae

When a giant star explodes in a big, bright supernova explosion, it creates a cloud called a planetary nebula. Gas and dust don't give off light, so how can you see nebulae? Some nebulae emit their own light from stars within. Others reflect the light of stars nearby. There are also dark nebulae, which are so dense they block out light. For example, the Coalsack Nebula is known for what you can't see: it blocks out a section of the Milky Way, and that dark, cloudy patch is how the nebula is known.

Cosmic pictures

Powerful telescopes have taken impressive photos of faraway nebulae. NASA's Hubble Space Telescope captured the Pillars of Creation in the Eagle Nebula.

Top 5 biggest nebulae known

1. NGC 262 Halo Cloud (span of over 1 million light years)
2. The Leo Ring (span of 650,000 light years)
3. The Magallenic Stream (span of 600,000 light years)
4. LAB-1 (span of 300,000 light years)
5. Himiko Gas Cloud (span of 55,000 light years)

TRUE OR FALSE? The letters in LAB-1 stand for Lyman-alpha blob. Find out on p.88!

PATTERNS IN THE STARS

For thousands of years, people have been finding patterns and telling stories in the stars.

Constellations

A constellation is a collection of stars that has been grouped together into a pattern, almost like a dot-to-dot picture in the sky. They are named after the person, object or animal that people see in the pattern. There are 88 official constellations.

By the stars

Constellations work as landmarks in the sky. For hundreds of years, sailors used these patterns to find well-known stars and determine their ship's location and direction on sea voyages. Nowadays, robotic spacecraft use constellations as markers in maps of the sky. Astronomers also use them to divide the night sky into 88 areas, each containing a constellation, and to track stars.

Hercules is a constellation representing the strong Greek hero.

The large constellation Leo represents a lion.

the Plough

Ursa Major →

Asterisms

Smaller patterns of stars in the sky are called asterisms. They form familiar shapes that help identify areas of the night sky. One of the most famous asterisms is the Big Dipper, or the Plough. It is a ladle shape (a large, round deep spoon with a long handle) in the larger constellation Ursa Major, the Great Bear.

FASCINATING FACT

Groups of shooting stars, known as meteor showers (see p.41), are named after the constellation they appear to come from. The Leonid shower, for example, looks to come from the constellation Leo!

Name that... CONSTELLATION

Concentrate on these constellations and see whether you can figure out which they all are. Shoot over to page 88 to see if you're right.

1
2
3

THE SOLAR SYSTEM

The solar system is the Sun and the group of planets, moons, asteroids and comets that revolve around it. Scientists used to think ours was the only planetary system like this in the universe, but now they know there are many more out there.

Our solar system

The solar system is Earth's home in space. It includes eight planets that orbit (go around) the Sun. Some of these planets have their own moons that orbit them. There are also thousands of comets and more than a million asteroids in the system. The gravity of the Sun keeps everything in position.

In the system

The four planets closest to the Sun (Mercury, Venus, Earth and Mars) are called the inner planets. The four planets beyond the asteroid belt are the outer planets (Jupiter, Saturn, Uranus and Neptune). At the far edge of the solar system is the Oort Cloud, a zone of icy objects thought to surround the entire solar system like a shell.

FASCINATING FACT

It took NASA's New Horizons spacecraft over nine years to travel from Earth to Pluto, a dwarf planet in the Kuiper Belt. It is now travelling deeper into the Kuiper Belt and will eventually leave the solar system altogether.

Saturn

Neptune

Uranus

THE SUN

Shining near the centre of the solar system is the big ball of hot gases that holds it all together: the Sun.

What is the Sun?

The Sun is an average-sized yellow dwarf star – a big ball of hydrogen and helium gases. It is the largest and heaviest object in the solar system by far, so its gravity pulls everything else towards it. This is why the planets and even pieces of debris stay in orbit, constantly swinging around the Sun.

Giving life

Not only is the Sun the only star in our solar system, but it is also the reason for the solar system. Without it, the objects wouldn't gather together – and life wouldn't exist on Earth! The Sun gives off heat and light energy that reaches the planet. Earth is just the right distance away from the Sun for plants to grow and creatures to survive.

Huge and hot

The Sun is a HUGE sphere – more than one million Earths could fit inside it! It is also extremely hot. Just the surface is a sizzling 5,600 °C. The core in the centre is about 15 million °C!

FASCINATING FACT

The Sun was born 4.6 billion years ago and is expected to live another 5 billion years.

ZOOM IN

A wispy outer atmosphere called the corona surrounds the Sun. It can reach temperatures as high as 2 million °C.

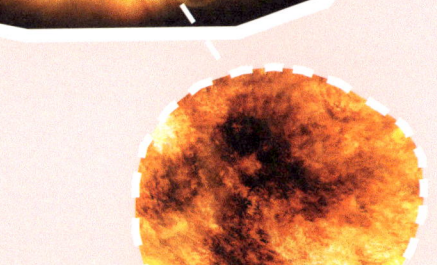

ZOOM IN

Sunspots are patches on the Sun's surface that appear to be dark and cool. But they are still very hot! They can disappear after a few weeks.

ZOOM IN

Explosions on the surface of the Sun cause energy to blast out in solar flares.

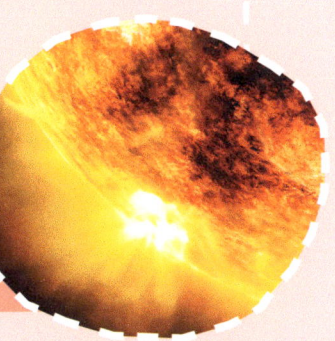

ECLIPSE OF THE SUN

The Sun is always there during the day, shining in the sky. But sometimes, on special occasions, it disappears for a few minutes, and the day goes dark. This is called a solar eclipse.

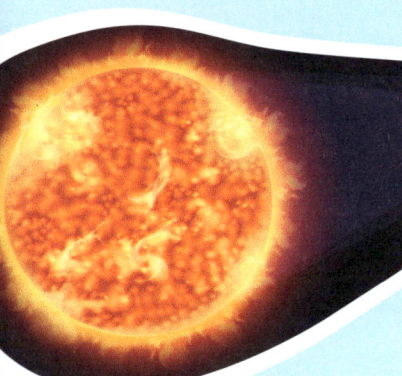

Solar eclipse

The Moon orbits around Earth, which orbits around the Sun. However, during a solar eclipse, the Sun, Moon and Earth line up exactly. This means the Moon blocks sunlight from reaching a part of Earth and it looks like nighttime! That part of Earth is in the Moon's shadow.

In the shadow

Looking at the eclipse from the shadowy area on Earth, scientists can see the Moon slowly cover the Sun. A blackness moves across until it hides the Sun completely. This is called the period of totality. However, the corona (the hot gassy atmosphere) can be seen glowing around the outside of the Sun.

Danger, danger!

It is never safe to look directly at the Sun. It is much too bright! During solar eclipses, people wear special eclipse glasses so they can safely observe what is happening.

FASCINATING FACT

The corona is not normally visible from Earth because the Sun's surface is so much brighter and outshines it. A total solar eclipse is the perfect time for it to come into view!

MERCURY

Mercury is the smallest and quickest planet in the solar system – and the closest to the Sun. This little planet is only slightly bigger than Earth's Moon!

Craters and core

The surface of Mercury is covered in craters made by the impact of collisions with asteroids and comets. At least one of these craters is bigger than the state of Texas, USA! Below the planet's outer shell is a large and dense core of metal. Mercury has no moons, no rings and a very thin atmosphere.

Zippy

Mercury zips around the Sun in only 88 days. Earth takes 365 days to make one full orbit.

So speedy!

Hot and cold

Because Mercury is so close to the Sun, it can get very hot in the day – up to 430°C! That's more than 25 times the average temperature on Earth. But there is only a very thin atmosphere on Mercury, so there is nothing to trap the heat and hold it in. At night temperatures plummet, and it can be as cold as -180 6th Feb 25°C. This means that in one day the temperature can vary by more than 600 6th Feb 25°C. That's the biggest temperature range of all planets in the solar system.

FASCINATING FACT

NASA's Messenger spacecraft was the first to orbit Mercury. It went around and around for more than four years, until it ran out of fuel and crashed into Mercury's surface.

Snowy surprise

Scientists believe there is ice made from water at Mercury's poles. This ice is hidden in deep, shaded areas where the Sun never reaches, so it doesn't melt.

VENUS

From the outside, wispy Venus looks calm and peaceful. But it is a hot, fiery planet surrounded by clouds of acid.

Heat trap

Although Venus isn't the closest planet to the Sun, it is the hottest. Its thick atmosphere traps the Sun's heat and keeps the surface at a sweltering 465°C. The surface of Venus is covered in spouting volcanoes and misshaped mountains.

Earth vs. Venus

Venus is sometimes described as Earth's evil twin. They are a similar size and both are rocky planets. However, the atmosphere on Venus is toxic and the pressure is much higher – enough to crush any unprotected visitors! Also, Venus has no moon.

Spinning tales

A day on Venus is a little longer than a year on Venus! This is because it takes 243 days for Venus to spin around on itself, but only 225 days for it to orbit the Sun. Venus also spins backwards (compared to most of the other planets), in the opposite direction to Earth.

Stink zone!

Got gas?

Surrounding Venus is a thick layer of toxic clouds. They are made of sulphuric acid droplets, which smell like rotten eggs!

5 hottest planets

1. Venus (465°C)
2. Mercury (430°C)
3. Earth (16°C)
4. Mars (-60°C)
5. Jupiter (-110°C)

FASCINATING FACT

The first spacecraft to land on another planet's surface landed on Venus. Because of the extreme heat, the lander didn't last long before it melted!

EARTH

Our home planet flourishes with water, air and life. It is the third planet from the Sun and one of the four rocky inner planets of the solar system.

Full of life!

Just right

Earth is in an area of space known as the Goldilocks Zone. It is not too far from the Sun and not too close either. It is just right! The temperature isn't too hot or cold, so liquid water can exist on the planet. This means life can exist too! With the perfect mix of water, air and sunlight, plants can thrive, and humans and other creatures can survive.

outer core

inner core

mantle

crust

On the inside

Earth is a rocky planet with four layers. On its surface is the crust, where living things exist. This layer has land and oceans. Below the crust is a hot layer of magma called the mantle. Then there is a liquid outer core and a solid metal inner core.

Spinning in space

Earth spins on its axis, an imaginary line that runs straight down from the North Pole to the South Pole. One full rotation takes 24 hours, or a day as you know it. While Earth is spinning, it is also moving slowly through space around the Sun. One full orbit takes 365 days, or one year. The Moon keeps Earth from wobbling too much as it spins.

Four seasons

Earth's axis is slightly tilted, which means that the planet is angled slightly in space. As it spins, different parts of the planet are closer to or further away from the Sun. This gives the planet four seasons: spring, summer, autumn and winter.

So much to see!

FASCINATING FACT

Nearly three-quarters of the surface of Earth is covered in water. There is so much of it, and some areas are so deep, that humans have explored only 5 per cent of the world's oceans!

THE MOON

Sticking with Earth in space is its closest neighbour, the Moon. The Moon orbits Earth as Earth orbits the Sun.

Moon make-up

Like Earth, the Moon has an outer rocky crust, a molten mantle and an inner metal core. The Moon is smaller than Earth – you could fit about four Moons across our home planet! The Moon's atmosphere is thin and weak, so the Moon is unprotected from sun radiation and asteroids. The surface is mainly grey, covered in dust and rocky debris.

ZOOM IN
The Moon's surface is covered in craters from hurtling asteroids and meteorites.

Phases of the Moon

The Moon produces no light of its own. Instead, it reflects light from the Sun, and this is how you see it in the sky. The Moon never changes shape, but it looks different from night to night because of where it is in its orbit in relation to Earth. These shapes are called the phases of the Moon. They range from a bright Full Moon to a dark New Moon – and back again!

New Moon | Waxing Crescent | First Quarter | Waxing Gibbous

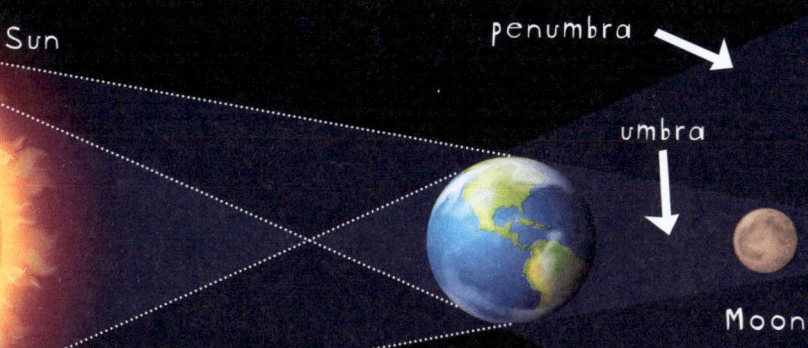

Lunar eclipse

A lunar eclipse happens when Earth gets in the way of the Sun's light hitting the Moon. This means that during the night, a Full Moon fades away because Earth's shadow covers it up. The umbra is where the Moon is completely in Earth's shadow and the penumbra is where the Moon is only partly in Earth's shadow. The Moon might look orange for a few hours because Earth's atmosphere absorbs the other colours as it bends sunlight towards the Moon.

FAMOUS FIGURE: Katherine Johnson

In 1969, history was made when the first humans stepped on the Moon. This mission would not have been possible without the help of a group of women working behind the scenes, including Katherine Johnson. Working at NASA, Johnson performed mathematical calculations that helped to plot the path for the Apollo 11 moon mission, sending the astronauts safely to the Moon and back. She was given the nickname 'human computer'!

Full Moon | Waning Gibbous | Third Quarter | Waning Crescent

MARS

The red planet is the planet most similar to Earth, but there are some key differences. Mainly, nobody lives there – yet!

Mars vs Earth

Mars is a rocky planet with mountains, polar ice caps, dried-up rivers and canyons, just like Earth. It even has its own seasons because of the tilt of its axis. The atmosphere is much thinner than Earth's and is made mainly of carbon dioxide, a gas that humans cannot breathe much of. Mars has two tiny moons: Phobos and Deimos.

FASCINATING FACT

Mars has iron oxide (rust) in the soil, which makes its surface look red. The ancient Romans named Mars after their god of war because the red colour reminded them of blood.

Robot explorers

Robotic rovers roam the red planet, taking photos and gathering samples to send back to Earth. Scientists believe that Mars used to be much warmer, with liquid water, and life could have existed on the planet then.

Working hard!

A new home

Scientists at NASA think that the first person who will step foot on Mars is alive right now! They hope to explore the planet in the near future and maybe one day set up a settlement there too. This would require a lot of preparation and special measures, such as spacesuits and covered buildings where humans could breathe.

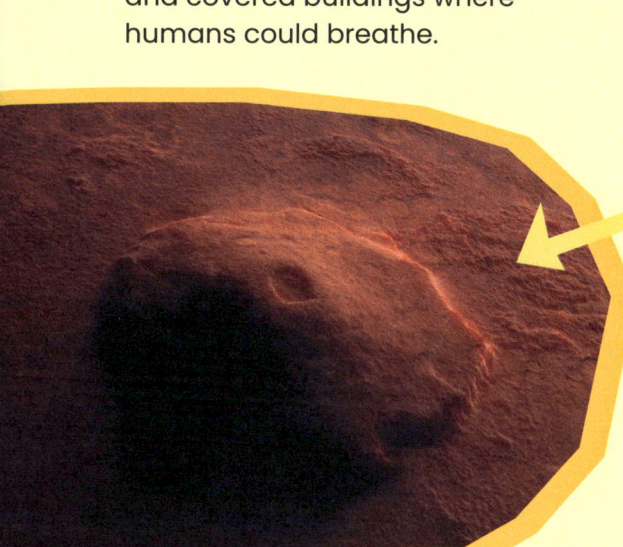

Olympus Mons

Record breaker

Mars is home to Olympus Mons, the tallest mountain in the entire solar system. This volcano stretches to about 25 km tall – that's three Mount Everests on top of each other!

5 tallest-known mountains in the solar system

1. Olympus Mons (25 km on Mars)
2. Rheasilvia Mons (20–25 km on the asteroid Vesta)
3. Equatorial Ridge (up to 20 km on Saturn's moon Iapetus)
4. Ascreaus Mons (up to 18 km on Mars)
5. Boösaule Montes (up to 17.5 km on Jupiter's moon Io)

Equatorial Ridge on Saturn's Iapetus

THE ASTEROID BELT

When the solar system formed 4.6 billion years ago, giant rocks were sent flying out into space. Most of these rocky and metallic objects now orbit the Sun in a ring known as the asteroid belt, located between Mars and Jupiter.

Big and small

The asteroid belt contains millions of space rocks of different sizes. They range from the big asteroids like Vesta, which is 530 km across, to small asteroids, only 10 metres across. Some asteroids are big enough to have their own orbiting moon (or two!). If you put all the asteroids in the asteroid belt together, their mass would be less than Earth's Moon.

FASCINATING FACT

NASA's NEAR Shoemaker spacecraft was the first spacecraft to not only orbit an asteroid but to land on one too.

Collision course

Asteroids rotate and tumble in space as they move around the Sun. Sometimes, asteroids can be knocked off course and sent out of the main belt completely, hurtling towards other objects and planets. Scientists are constantly monitoring asteroids close to Earth to make sure they won't crash into the planet.

Epic journey

Sometimes pieces of asteroid smash into each other and break off. When they continue to orbit the Sun, they are called meteoroids. However, if the meteoroid is knocked off course and enters Earth's atmosphere, it is called a meteor. These meteors glow in the atmosphere and are what you might see as shooting stars. Finally, if the meteor makes it all the way to Earth's surface, it is called a meteorite.

meteorite

meteoroid

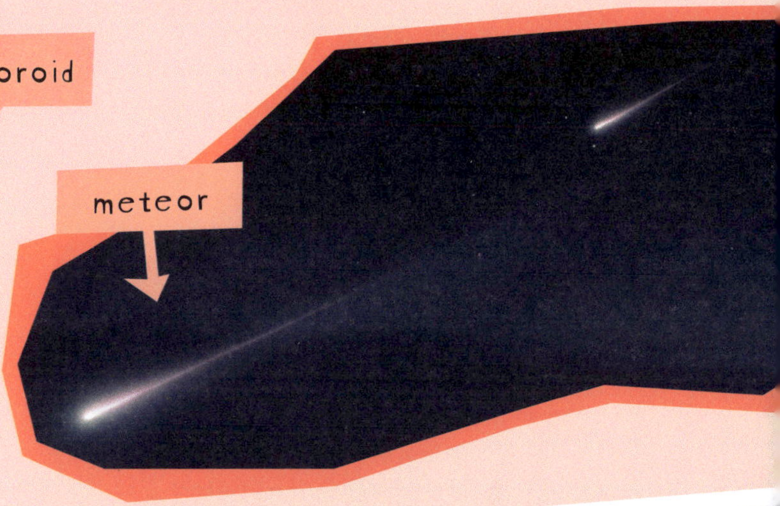

meteor

Super Stats

COMETS AND METEOR SHOWERS

Comets are chunks of dirty ice orbiting the Sun. As they near the Sun, they warm up and trail a tail of gas and dust particles. We can see these comets as they fly past Earth.

First repeat comet

Halley's Comet was the first repeat or periodic comet, meaning that it returns to Earth again and again. In 1705, astronomer Edmond Halley discovered that comets that had been sighted every 76 years were in fact the same comet. This discovery helped scientists realise that comets orbit the Sun – going round and coming back again!

Largest comet discovered

The Bernardinelli-Bernstein Comet is estimated to have a core 128 km across. That's about 50 times bigger than the average comet.

Shortest orbital period

The Encke Comet orbits the Sun every 3.3 years.

When Earth passes through the dusty debris of a comet or asteroid (see pp.38–39), it creates a spectacular show of many shooting stars called a meteor shower.

 **Most meteors**

The Perseid meteor shower can produce up to 100 meteors every hour at its peak point. It is one of the best-known meteor showers for its bright and frequent meteors soaring across the sky.

 **Fastest meteors**

The Leonid meteors move as fast as 71 km per second.

 **Most brilliant meteor shower**

In November 1833, a Leonid meteor shower gave a spectacular display of tens of thousands of meteors in just four hours.

 **Famous meteor showers**

1. Quadrantid (January)
2. Eta Aquarid (May)
3. Perseid (July/August)
4. Orionid (October)
5. Leonid (November)
6. Geminid (December)

JUPITER

The largest planet in the solar system by far, Jupiter is more than twice as massive as all the other planets put together!

First on the block

Jupiter was the first planet to form in the solar system after the Sun, 4.6 billion years ago. This planet has the fastest rotation of all planets too – it spins around on its axis in just 10 hours. That's so fast that the planet bulges out at the middle from the speed.

Swirling surface

Jupiter is a gas planet, with no solid surface that you could land on. Thick gas clouds in the atmosphere swirl above a liquid hydrogen ocean. Below that is likely to be a small metal core. Jupiter is made mostly of hydrogen and helium – the same gases as the Sun – but is a very cold, windy, stormy place!

Bands and rings

Because Jupiter spins so fast, its clouds have spread out into clear bands. These move at different speeds and in different directions. Jupiter has very faint rings of dust too.

ZOOM IN

The Great Red Spot is a giant storm on Jupiter that has been raging for more than three hundred years. It is roughly twice the size of Earth!

Ganymede

Many moons

Jupiter has 95 moons! One of its moons, Ganymede, is the largest moon in the entire solar system – even bigger than the planet Mercury! Another moon called Io has the most active volcanoes in the solar system.

FAMOUS FIGURE: Galileo Galilei

In 1610, Italian astronomer Galileo Galilei spotted four fascinating objects in the night sky: Jupiter's four largest moons! These were Ganymede, Io, Europa and Callisto. Using a very early telescope, Galileo was the first person to discover moons orbiting a planet other than Earth. This discovery helped prove that not everything in the solar system revolved around Earth. During his lifetime, Galileo made many other contributions to astronomy and science in general.

SATURN

One of the gas giants, Saturn is the second-largest planet in the solar system. It is best known for its magnificent rings.

Gas giant

Saturn is made mostly of the gases hydrogen and helium. Like Jupiter, it has no solid surface, so spacecraft can't land on it. It has liquid deep below the surface, and a metallic core which is probably slushy. A massive rotating storm rages at Saturn's north pole.

Gathering data

NASA's Cassini spacecraft orbited the planet for 13 years. Along with the Huygens probe, which landed on Saturn's largest moon, Titan, it gathered photos and data and sent these back to Earth, for scientists to learn more about this fascinating member of the solar system.

Cassini spacecraft

Rings

Other planets have rings too, but Saturn's are the most vast and visible. There are seven main rings orbiting the planet, with a gap between each one. All together, the rings are more than double the width of Saturn itself.

FASCINATING FACT

There is a large gap – about 4,800 km – between two rings of Saturn called the Cassini Division. It was named after the Italian astronomer who discovered the gap – Giovanni Domenico Cassini.

ZOOM IN

Saturn's rings are made of a mixture of tiny specks of dust and huge chunks of ice as big as mountains.

Saturn stats

A day on Saturn lasts only about ten and a half hours, but a year on Saturn is the equivalent of about 29 years on Earth. Saturn has the most moons of all planets in the solar system. A whopping 146 moons have been discovered so far!

FASCINATING FACT

Saturn is the furthest planet from Earth that was discovered with the unaided eye – no telescope needed!

URANUS

The first of the two ice giants, Uranus is windy and very cold. From afar, Uranus is a calm and peaceful blue. But what secrets lie within?

One of a kind...

Rings and moons

Uranus has 13 faint rings surrounding it, which can be seen with a powerful telescope, spacecraft and thermal imaging. It also has 28 known moons.

On its side

Uranus is unique! It is the only planet that appears to spin on its side, with its axis tilted over 90 degrees. Not only that, but this planetary giant spins backwards, in the opposite direction to Earth. Uranus and Venus are the only two planets to do this.

TRUE OR FALSE? Some of Uranus's moons are named after characters from plays by William Shakespeare. Find out on p.88!

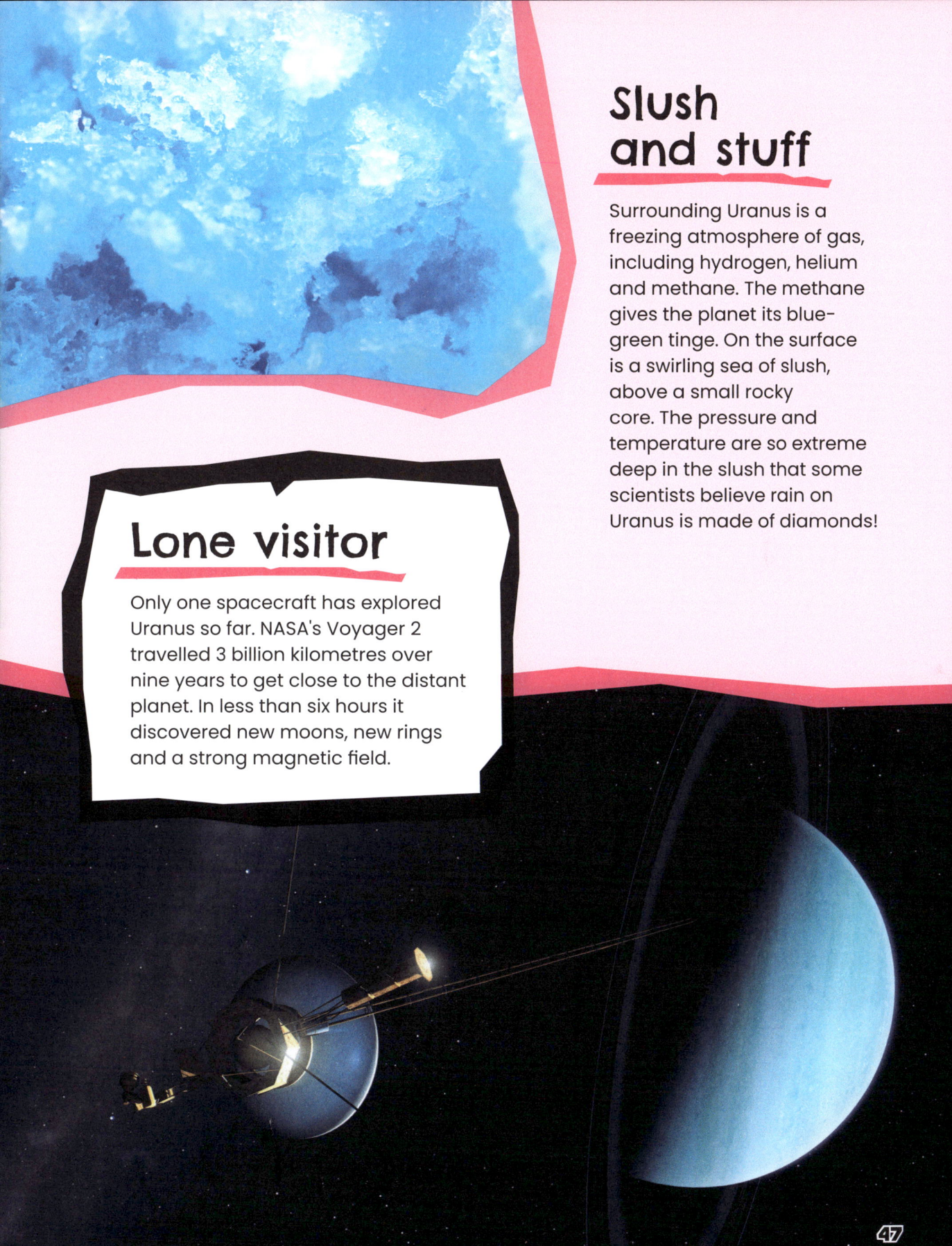

Slush and stuff

Surrounding Uranus is a freezing atmosphere of gas, including hydrogen, helium and methane. The methane gives the planet its blue-green tinge. On the surface is a swirling sea of slush, above a small rocky core. The pressure and temperature are so extreme deep in the slush that some scientists believe rain on Uranus is made of diamonds!

Lone visitor

Only one spacecraft has explored Uranus so far. NASA's Voyager 2 travelled 3 billion kilometres over nine years to get close to the distant planet. In less than six hours it discovered new moons, new rings and a strong magnetic field.

NEPTUNE

The furthest planet from the Sun, Neptune is last but not at all least. The strongest winds in the solar system thrash about and whip frozen clouds around at superspeed.

Hot and cold

Neptune is the second of the two planets known as ice giants. Like Uranus, methane gas in Neptune's atmosphere gives the planet a blue hue. Neptune also has a small rocky core. Scientists believe that a hot ocean might be lurking under the planet's cold clouds.

Dim Sun

Neptune is 30 times farther from the Sun than Earth is. In the middle of the day on Neptune, the Sun would be only as bright as it is at twilight here on Earth. Put another way, the Sun is about 900 times brighter on Earth than it is on Neptune!

Seasons change

Neptune is tilted towards the Sun in a similar way to Earth, so this planet has seasons similar to Earth. However, these seasons last much longer – over 40 years each!

FASCINATING FACT

In 1989, a storm called the Great Dark Spot raged on Neptune. It was big enough to contain all of planet Earth!

Triton

Of Neptune's 16 known moons, Triton is the largest. It has an icy surface and a rocky core. It is also unusual for the big moons in the solar system: it travels in the opposite direction to the way Neptune rotates.

Triton

Neptune

5 biggest moons in the solar system

1. Ganymede (Jupiter)
2. Titan (Saturn)
3. Callisto (Jupiter)
4. Io (Jupiter)
5. Moon (Earth)

Titan – one of Saturn's moons

Name that... PLANET

How well do you remember your planets? Check here and then rocket over to page 90 to see if you got them right!

1

2

3

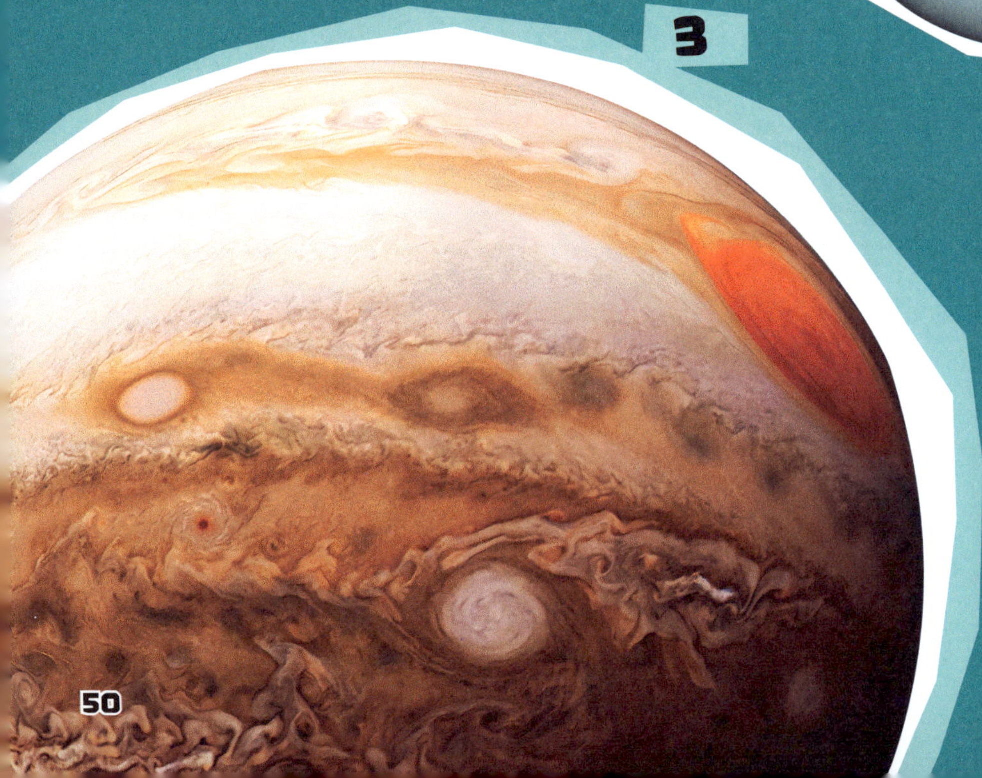

DWARF PLANETS

As well as the eight planets in the solar system, five dwarf planets orbit the Sun. They are similar to planets but smaller than them.

Pluto

The most famous dwarf planet is Pluto, which was classed as the solar system's ninth planet until 2006. Pluto is smaller than Earth's moon and has five moons of its own. Its largest one, Charon, is half the size of Pluto itself! Pluto and Charon orbit each other like a double planet.

Charon

Pluto

ZOOM IN

In 2015, NASA's New Horizons spacecraft flew past Pluto and discovered a heart shape on its surface.

Ceres

The only dwarf planet in the inner solar system, Ceres has the honour of being the largest object in the asteroid belt between Mars and Jupiter. It is different from most other asteroids in the belt – much bigger and much more like a planet than a rock.

Haumea

This planet rotates so quickly that it is shaped like a rugby ball rather than a round ball. It is found in the distant Kuiper Belt (see pp.54–55), is extremely cold and has two known moons. It was the first object in the Kuiper Belt known to have rings.

Makemake

After Pluto, dwarf planet Makemake is the second brightest object in the Kuiper Belt. It is slightly smaller than Pluto – and one of the reasons Pluto was declassified as a planet. After Makemake was discovered in 2005, astronomers defined the group of smaller planets now known as dwarf planets.

Makemake

Eris

Along with Makemake, the discovery of Eris in 2005 pushed scientists to define dwarf planets. Eris is similar in size to Pluto and also found in the Kuiper Belt.

Eris

FASCINATING FACT

There are five dwarf planets known – so far! Scientists think there might be many more out there, waiting to be discovered.

THE KUIPER BELT

Beyond the orbit of Neptune lies a doughnut-shaped ring of millions of icy objects, some comets and most of the dwarf planets too. This is known as the Kuiper Belt (pronounced 'KY-purr').

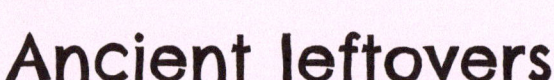

Ancient leftovers

Like the asteroid belt (see pp.38–39), the Kuiper Belt is made of objects left over from when the solar system formed billions of years ago. It wraps around the Sun in a huge, thick disc.

Famous objects

Objects discovered in this area are called Kuiper Belt Objects (KBOs). The dwarf planet Pluto is probably the most famous of these, but Eris, Haumea and Makemake are found there too (see pp.52–53). Another famous KBO is Arrokoth: a small snowman-shaped object a billion miles beyond Pluto. It is the farthest object explored by a spacecraft.

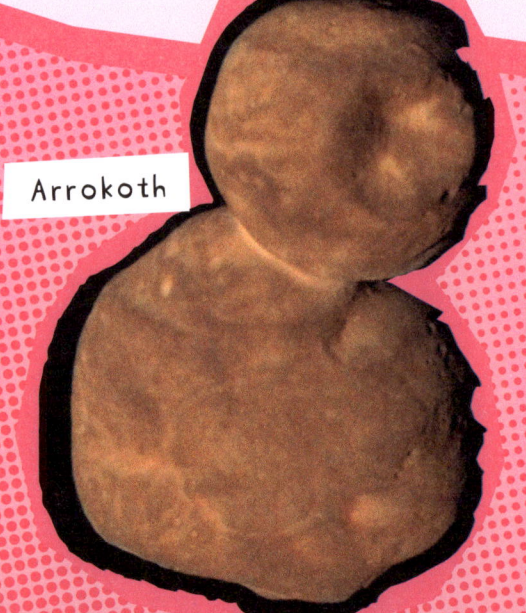

Arrokoth

FASCINATING FACT

Scientists have so far named more than 2000 large Kuiper Belt Objects. But they believe there are more than 100,000 others!

Comet factory

When objects in the Kuiper Belt collide, they can be bumped out of the belt and into their own orbit towards the Sun. These can become comets.

Lots to learn

Much of the Kuiper Belt is still a mystery to scientists. It is so vast, and they've only just started to explore it. The New Horizons spacecraft is journeying through at this very moment, collecting new data and photos to share.

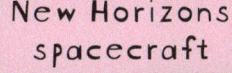

New Horizons spacecraft

THE OORT CLOUD

Way beyond the Kuiper Belt, even further out in deep space, lies an even bigger area of icy chunks! This sphere is known as the Oort Cloud.

Super shell

Scientists believe that the Oort Cloud surrounds the entire solar system like a giant sphere-shaped shell. Space debris floats around in a thick bubble containing trillions of objects. Some of these icy pieces can be as big as mountains!

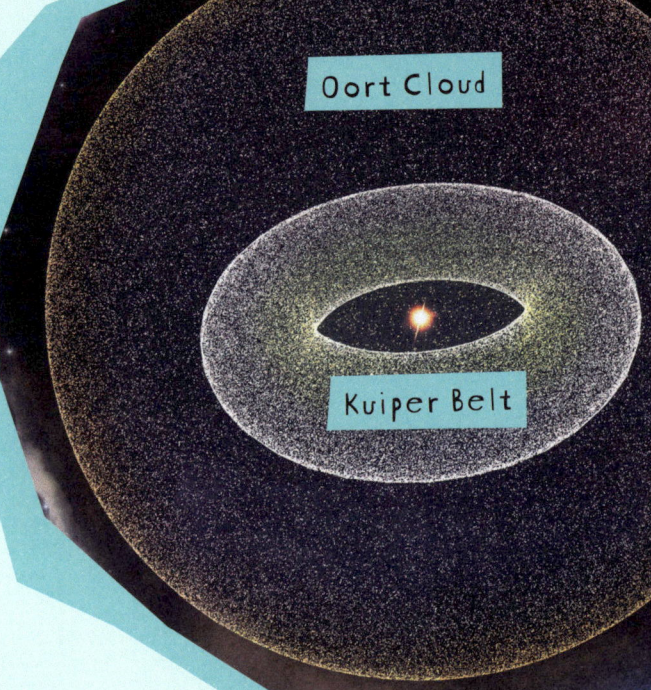

Long journey

Just as they come from the Kuiper Belt (see pp.54-55), comets come from the Oort Cloud too. But they travel for much longer! These comets can take hundreds of thousands of years to orbit the Sun.

Oort Cloud

Sun · Mercury · Venus · Earth · Mars · Jupiter · Saturn · Uranus · Neptune

Mystery cloud

Nobody has actually seen the Oort Cloud. It is so far away that the nearest spacecraft won't reach it for another 300 years! Scientists believe it exists because of the long-orbiting comets that have been observed passing Earth. These might be proof that they've come from this mysterious faraway place.

TRUE OR FALSE? Once the Voyager 1 spacecraft reaches the Oort Cloud, it will take 30,000 years to get through it. Find out on p.88!

Outer edge

The Oort Cloud is at the very edge of our solar system. It is the last place where the Sun has any pull on objects, or provides any light or heat. Beyond that is interstellar space.

EXOPLANETS

Any planet outside of our solar system is called an exoplanet. More than 5800 exoplanets have been identified, but scientists believe billions of them exist across the universe.

Milky Way and beyond

Most of the exoplanets discovered so far have been in our very own Milky Way galaxy. The closest exoplanet to Earth is called Proxima Centauri b. It is about four lightyears away, which is over 20 trillion miles.

All sorts and sizes

FASCINATING FACT
There are more planets than stars in the Milky Way galaxy. This is because each star probably has at least one planet orbiting it – maybe more!

Just like the planets in the solar system, exoplanets vary from one to the next. Some are rocky like Earth and some are gas planets like Jupiter. They can be mostly water, ice, metal or even hot lava.

To orbit or not

The orbits of these exoplanets can vary widely too. Some of them might go around their star in just a few hours or days, while others might take thousands of years. Scientists have even discovered exoplanets that orbit two stars at the same time. And would you believe there are exoplanets with no orbit at all? Instead of circling a star, they float through the galaxy freely, in total darkness.

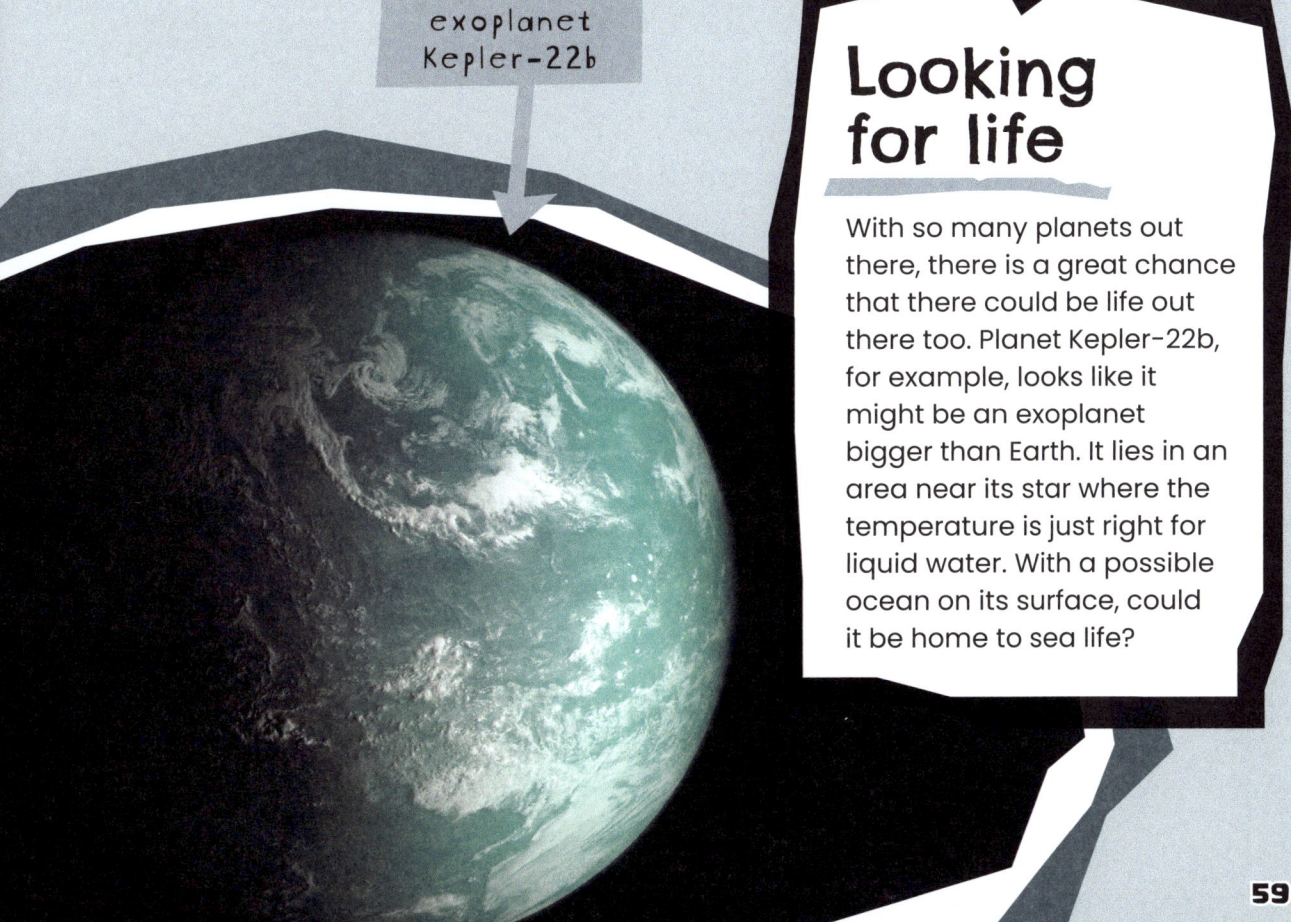

exoplanet Kepler-22b

Looking for life

With so many planets out there, there is a great chance that there could be life out there too. Planet Kepler-22b, for example, looks like it might be an exoplanet bigger than Earth. It lies in an area near its star where the temperature is just right for liquid water. With a possible ocean on its surface, could it be home to sea life?

BLACK HOLES

Black holes are one of the universe's greatest mysteries. There is a lot that scientists don't know about them. But what do they know so far?

Not a hole

Black holes are not holes at all. They're actually incredibly dense clusters of matter, packed into a tiny space. The area just within the black hole has such a strong gravitational pull that nothing can escape – not even light! This is why they look black.

FASCINATING FACT

Sometimes, rings of gas and dust that surround black holes give off light. This helps scientists detect where black holes might be.

Tell me more...

Some black holes are formed when massive stars collapse in a supernova explosion. All black holes spin in place. When matter gets too close to a black hole, it is squeezed horizontally and stretched vertically, so it looks like a noodle or a piece of spaghetti! This process is called spaghettification.

Sagittarius A*

Right at the centre of the Milky Way galaxy lies a humongous black hole, four million times more massive than the Sun. Stars in the galaxy orbit around it. It is thought that all other galaxies have at least one black hole at their centre too.

Ruby Payne-Scott

FAMOUS FIGURE

Australian physicist Ruby Payne-Scott was the first female astronomer to work with radio waves: invisible waves of radiation that travel through space with a specific frequency that can be detected. Her work led to the discovery of solar bursts – and black holes! Later, this work helped scientists learn how solar storms can affect weather in space and even disrupt electrical systems on Earth.

Quiz Yourself On...

OBJECTS IN SPACE

Check your answers on p.88!

Do you know your meteors from your meteorites? Could you pick out a planet in a line-up? Put your knowledge of the various objects in space to the test...

1 What do you call a scientist who studies space?

   A. an astronomer
   B. a geologist
   C. a zoologist

2 How old is the universe?

   A. 13.8 million years old
   B. 13.8 billion years old
   C. 13.8 trillion years old

3 What is the name of the galaxy that is home to our solar system?

   A. the Andromeda Galaxy
   B. the Milky Way
   C. the Tadpole Galaxy

4 What is the longest stage of a star's life?

   A. main sequence
   B. nebula
   C. supernova

TRUE OR FALSE? On Mars, the daytime sky is blue and the sunset looks red. *Find out on p.88!*

5 How many planets are in the solar system?
- A. 5
- B. 8
- C. 10

6 What is the hottest planet in the solar system?
- A. Mercury
- B. Venus
- C. Jupiter

7 Earth can support life because it sits in the...
- A. Cinderella Zone
- B. Goldilocks Zone
- C. Living Zone

8 What was a nickname for Katherine Johnson?
- A. human computer
- B. human smartphone
- C. human telescope

9 When a piece of asteroid reaches Earth's surface, it is called a...
- A. meteoroid
- B. meteor
- C. meteorite

10 What lies at the very edge of our solar system?
- A. Pluto
- B. the Kuiper Belt
- C. the Oort Cloud

SPACE TRAVEL

Humans have been fascinated by space for thousands of years, but travelling into space to see celestial sights up close is a relatively recent discovery.

Space shuttles

Space shuttles are spacecraft that can be used over and over again. They have wings and rockets, and fuel tanks and oxygen tanks that give the shuttle a powerful boost through the Earth's atmosphere. When all the fuel has been used in a space shuttle's boosters, the boosters fall into the ocean and can be recovered by humans. At the end of a mission, the shuttle returns to Earth and lands just like an aeroplane.

Discovery

A well-known shuttle was Discovery, which put the Hubble Space Telescope into orbit around Earth. This telescope takes photos of space and sends them back via radio waves to astronomers and scientists on Earth. These photos play a very important role in space research.

Major moments

4 OCTOBER 1957
First artificial satellite launched: *Sputnik 1*

31 JANUARY 1958
First US satellite launched: *Explorer 1*

12 APRIL 1961
Russian Yuri Gagarin became the first human to go to space

16 JUNE 1963
Russian Valentina Tereshkova became the first woman to go to space

Space stations

Space stations are spacecraft that stay in orbit for long periods of time. Scientists can spend weeks or months living in them doing experiments. Conditions in space that are hard to recreate on Earth – like zero gravity and extreme temperatures – are at the heart of their investigations.

FAMOUS FIGURE: Mae Carol Jemison

In September 1992, doctor and engineer Mae Carol Jemison became the first Black woman to go into space. She travelled on Space Shuttle Endeavour, on mission STS-47, spending over 190 hours in space and orbiting Earth 127 times!

20 JULY 1969
American Neil Armstrong became the first human to walk on the Moon

24 APRIL 1990
The Space Shuttle Discovery put the Hubble Space Telescope into orbit around Earth

12 APRIL 1981
US launched first space shuttle

6 DECEMBER 1998
Assembly of the International Space Station (ISS) began

2 NOVEMBER 2000
First crew started living in the ISS

LOOKING INTO SPACE

In the past, humans could only look at space with their eyes. Over time, people developed telescopes that helped them get a closer look. These special instruments got bigger and better, and now there are even telescopes that work in space itself!

Early telescopes

In 1608, Hans Lippershey, a spectacle maker in the Netherlands, revealed the first special lens that could make things appear closer than they actually were. In 1609, English astronomer Thomas Harriot used his own telescope to view the Moon close up. In the same year, Italian astronomer Galileo Galilei (see p.43) made a telescope that he turned to the skies and used for many major discoveries about the solar system.

How they work

A telescope is a device used to make faraway objects look closer. It uses a series of mirrors to reflect light from space and enlarge the picture for your eye. Special telescopes called radio telescopes use radio waves to make pictures of things that the human eye can't see.

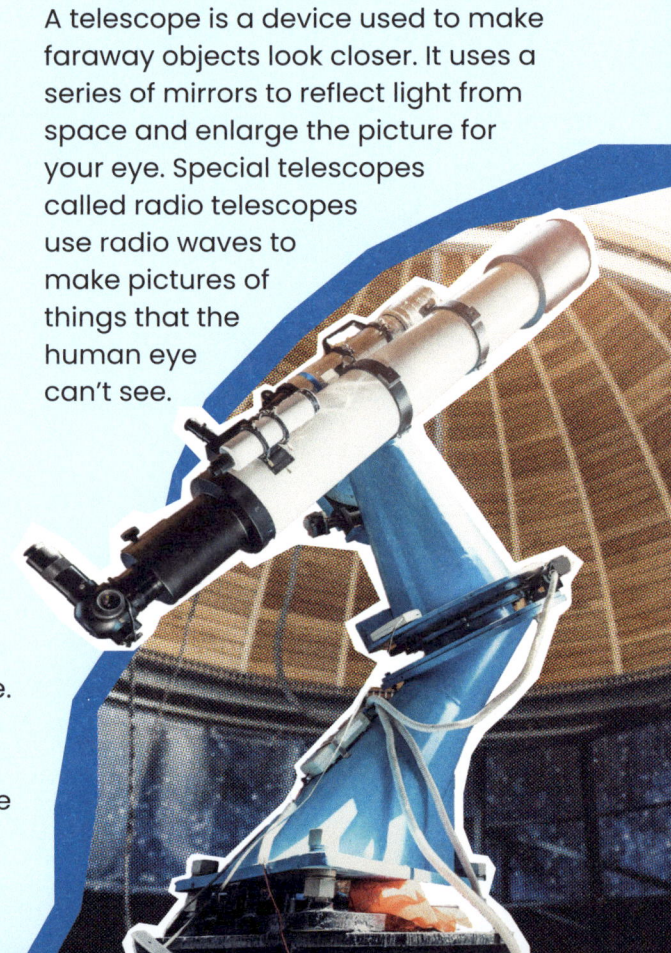

Modern telescopes

Giant telescopes in ground-based observatories get great views into space. Often built on a high hill or mountain, observatories are away from city lights and where the air is clear. Their large size allows them to look far into space.

FASCINATING FACT

Large telescopes at the W.M. Keck Observatory in Hawaii can see moving stars in neighbouring galaxy Andromeda! These twin telescopes sit above the clouds on a dormant volcano.

Good view!

Telescopes in space

Where better to view the universe than from space itself? In 1990, the first telescope was launched into orbit – and it is still there today! The Hubble Space Telescope orbits Earth, high up where its view out to space isn't distorted by the atmosphere. It takes pictures of planets and moons within our solar system, distant stars and galaxies billions of lightyears away.

Ask an EXPERT about... THE NORTHERN LIGHTS

This is Tom Kerss, professional astronomer and aurora chaser! Tom was five years old when he first saw the Northern Lights, and he's been fascinated by space and astronomy ever since.

What are the Northern Lights?

The Northern Lights are spectacular light displays in the northern hemisphere's night sky, visible in the Arctic between September and March. Different coloured lights, including green, red and pink – and rarely blue or purple – appear in swirls and ribbons, dancing across huge sections of the sky.

What causes them?

The Northern Lights are also known as 'aurora borealis'. 'Aurora' refers to the displays of lights, and 'borealis' means 'northerly'. Auroras form when particles flowing out from the Sun become trapped inside the Earth's magnetic field. This gives the particles a huge amount of energy, and as they plunge down into the atmosphere near the magnetic poles, they give that energy to gas atoms and molecules high above us, causing them to glow.

Tell us something unusual about the Northern Lights!

Did you know that, very occasionally, the Northern Lights can make noise? Scientists think that when static in the air builds up on very still nights, it sometimes makes a crackling sound!

TOP 5 PLACES TO SEE THE NORTHERN LIGHTS

1. Tromsø, Norway
2. Alaska, USA
3. Kiruna, Swedish Lapland
4. Reykjavik, Iceland
5. Rovaniemi, Finnish Lapland

SATELLITES

Humans launch lots of machines into space to help them dig deeper into the wonders of the universe. Some of these devices help scientists to learn more about life on Earth, while others gather information about the worlds beyond our home planet.

Natural or artificial

Satellites are objects that orbit a planet or star. The moon is a satellite because it orbits Earth, and Earth is a satellite because it orbits the Sun! They are natural satellites. Human-made satellites are known as artificial satellites. There are thousands of artificial satellites orbiting Earth right now.

Looking down

Some satellites look down to Earth. For example, weather satellites get a good, wide view from above. They can gather information to help meteorologists (people who study the weather and climate) predict the weather and track climate changes. Communication satellites receive and send signals back to Earth, to carry TV signals and phone calls around the world. A group of navigation satellites works together to pinpoint exact positions of GPS (Global Positioning System) receivers on Earth. This helps people know where they are and prevents them from getting lost.

Looking out

Some satellites look out towards the stars. Orbiting above Earth's atmosphere, they can gather clear photos and data about planets, black holes and distant galaxies. Antennas on the satellites help them to send and receive information. There are even some satellites orbiting planets further into space.

FASCINATING FACT

The very first artificial satellite launched into space was just the size of a basketball. Sputnik 1 orbited Earth for three months.

ROCKETS

Earth has such a powerful gravity that most objects that go up come back down again. If they are travelling at just the right speed, they might get into orbit and become satellites (see pp.70–71). It takes a huge amount of energy to propel an object to the point of orbit or beyond, where it can escape the pull of Earth's gravity entirely. This is where rockets come in.

Rocket science

A rocket carries another spacecraft into space. This could take the spacecraft into orbit or deeper into space. The further the spacecraft needs to go, the more powerful the rocket! To produce enough energy to blast off, fuel is burned inside the rocket. Gas from the rocket engine is pushed backwards out of the rocket, which in turn pushes on the rocket and propels it forwards. This force is called thrust.

Lift off!

This rocket is made of two parts. The capsule at the top carries the crew (buckled in tight!), as well as essentials such as batteries and solar panels. This capsule sits on the rocket, which carries the capsule into space. After lift-off, the two parts separate. The rocket returns to Earth while the capsule carries on.

Through the years

The very first rockets were invented in China in the 1200s and might sound familiar... they were fireworks! These rockets were powered by gunpowder explosions and were used for fancy displays as well as weapons. Over time, scientists developed bigger and more powerful rockets to reach for the stars. In 1969, the first astronauts stepped foot on the moon thanks to the rocket Saturn V. This huge rocket was taller than the Statue of Liberty!

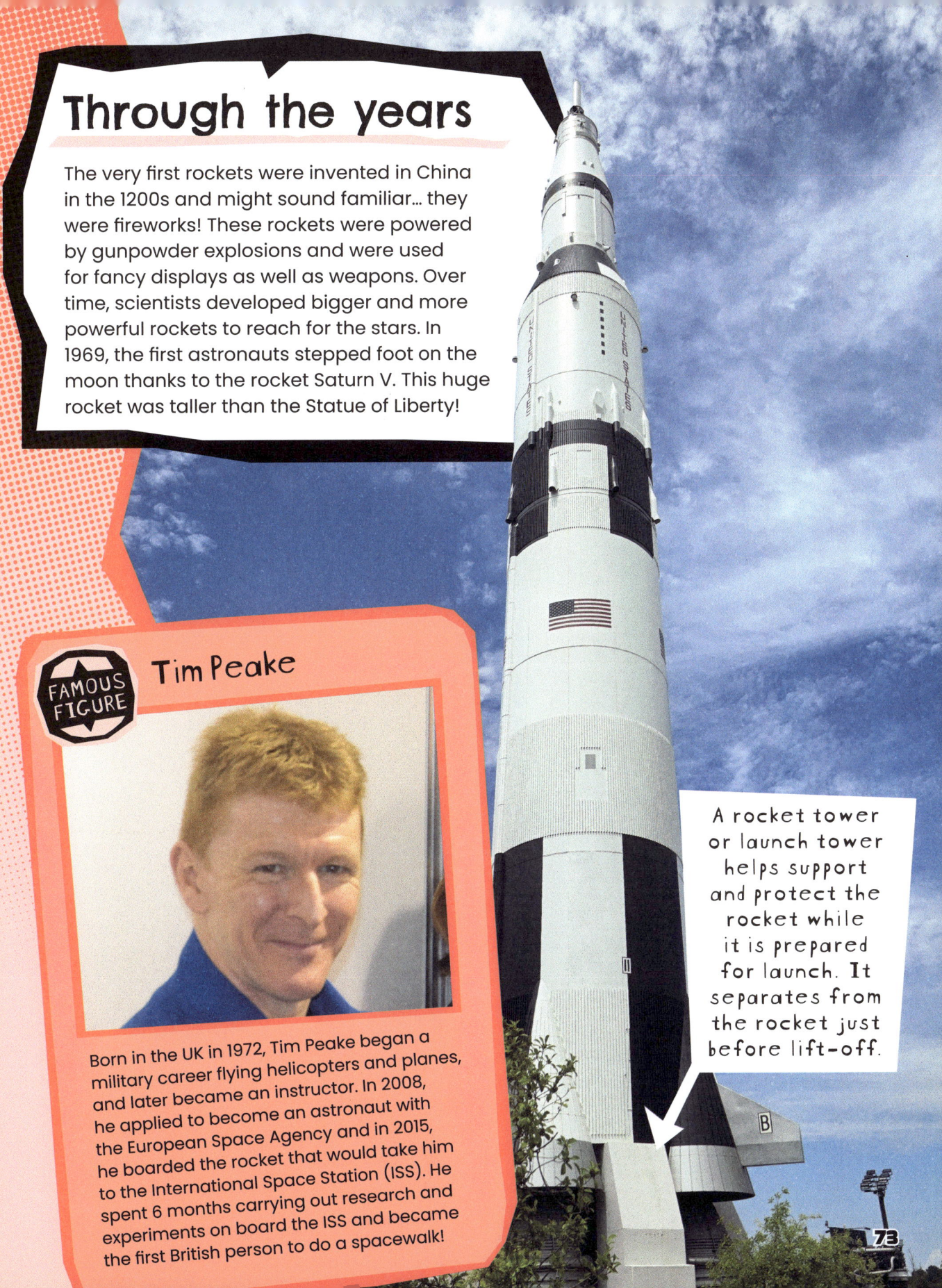

FAMOUS FIGURE: Tim Peake

Born in the UK in 1972, Tim Peake began a military career flying helicopters and planes, and later became an instructor. In 2008, he applied to become an astronaut with the European Space Agency and in 2015, he boarded the rocket that would take him to the International Space Station (ISS). He spent 6 months carrying out research and experiments on board the ISS and became the first British person to do a spacewalk!

A rocket tower or launch tower helps support and protect the rocket while it is prepared for launch. It separates from the rocket just before lift-off.

THE INTERNATIONAL SPACE STATION

Circling the planet, high above you, astronauts live and work on the International Space Station (ISS).

Team effort

Like it says in the name, the ISS is an international effort. People from the US, Canada, Japan, Russia, Europe and other countries contributed parts needed to build the ISS. Astronauts from across the world live on the station together.

FASCINATING FACT
The ISS moves quite speedily, travelling around the world 16 times every 24 hours. The astronauts see a sunrise or a sunset every 45 minutes!

Living in space

Astronauts usually live on the ISS for up to six months at a time, and up to ten people live there at once. In the space station they are weightless and float around. Everything else is weightless too – including books, tools and drops of water!

Working in space

The space station is like a giant laboratory in space. Astronauts carry out experiments to test things such as how vegetables grow in zero gravity and how living in space affects humans. They can study Earth from above too.

Cosmic cosy!

Space walk

Sometimes, astronauts venture out from the space station to perform jobs outside. To do these space walks, they need to wear special spacesuits so they can breathe and keep warm.

Space junk

Space junk, or space debris, is items left by humans in space. This can include bits of rocket, tools that astronauts drop on space walks and even flecks of paint. There are millions of pieces of space debris of varying sizes. Some of these burn up as they enter Earth's atmosphere. Others are moving so quickly in orbit that they could cause problems if they hit satellites in space.

5 strange things floating in space

1. Camera belonging to astronaut Sunita Williams
2. Tool bag containing a scraper, bags for debris and other items
3. Needle-nose pliers from a 2007 spacewalk, when an astronaut was doing repairs
4. Astronaut Piers Sellers' favourite spatula
5. Frozen crystals of astronaut wee

ROVERS

While telescopes and satellites can study worlds from afar, scientists have developed special rovers that can land on the surface of Mars to study it up close. Since 1997, five different rovers have explored the red planet.

Roaming rovers

Rovers have wheels and can drive around to explore. They take samples of the rocky surface to test which materials and chemicals make it up. Searching for water and signs of life, the rovers provide data to help determine whether humans could one day visit and live on this neighbouring planet.

Long distance

Rovers travel very slowly across the terrain but explore for a number of years at a time. The rover named Opportunity spent nearly 15 years working on Mars. In that time, it travelled more than 45 km – the furthest of all landers on Mars and on the Moon too.

Looking for life

In 2021, the Perseverance rover landed on Mars. Its mission is to search for signs of ancient life on the planet. The previous rover, Curiosity, tested samples on board. Perseverance uses a robotic arm to collect samples to potentially be taken back to Earth for further study. Perseverance is about the size of a car.

ZOOM IN

Cameras mounted on the rover take pictures of the surroundings to send back to Earth.

5 Mars rover landings

1. Sojourner, 1997
2. Spirit and...
3. ... Opportunity, 2004
4. Curiosity, 2012
5. Perseverance, 2021

Perseverance on display in the Kennedy Space Centre in Florida, US

SPACE PROBES

At the moment, humans can travel only so far in space. They have reached the Moon and the ISS... but beyond that, it's up to machines to take over the research and exploration. Space probes are devices sent into space without human pilots.

FASCINATING FACT

Since the 1950s, more than 200 space probes have been sent into space.

Major moments

1957
Sputnik 1 was the very first space probe to enter space.

1959
The first spacecraft, Luna 2, reached the Moon.

1965
The first images of another planet (Mars) were captured by spacecraft Mariner 4.

1970
Venera 7 was the first spacecraft to land on another planet (Venus).

Intrepid explorers

Space probes are full of scientific tools, instruments and cameras to gather data on their journeys. Some of them travel to deep space to see what's out there, while others orbit or even land on planets or moons to study what they're made of. Some probes bring samples back to Earth for scientists to study. Others send data back by radio waves and never return home.

Cassini spacecraft approaching Saturn

1977
Voyager 1 and Voyager 2 launched into space. Since then they have taken photos of Jupiter, Saturn, Uranus and Neptune, and Voyager 1 has become the first probe to enter interstellar space.

1997
The Cassini spacecraft launched. It orbited Saturn and dropped a lander called Huygens on Saturn's biggest moon.

2014
The Philae probe was the first spacecraft to successfully land on a comet.

1990
The Hubble Space Telescope entered space and began to take incredible photos of faraway galaxies and supernovae.

2009
Kepler launched into deep space with a mission to discover new planets.

Super Stats

SPACE MISSIONS

The desire to study space has encouraged many incredible record-breaking missions.

Furthest space probe

NASA's Voyager 1 spacecraft is currently billions of kilometres from Earth, in interstellar space. This is the farthest any human-made object has travelled so far.

First people on the Moon

In July 1969, two astronauts made history. Arriving by spaceflight Apollo 11, Neil Armstrong and Edwin ('Buzz') Aldrin were the first people to ever step foot on the Moon. Their footprints are likely still there today.

First crew on the ISS

In November 2000, a crew of three international members became the first people to live on the International Space Station. American William Shepherd and Russians Yuri Gidzenko and Sergei Krikalev lived and worked there for four months before returning home.

Super speed

To enter Earth's orbit, rockets need to be travelling at about 28,000 km/h. If the rocket wants to escape Earth's gravity, it needs to go even faster: over 40,000 km/h!

Longest trip

Valeri Polyakov holds the record for the longest time spent in space in a single trip by a human. He spent 437 days straight in space!

Planet landings

Apart from Earth, uncrewed spacecraft have so far landed on only two planets: Venus and Mars. People have set foot on the Moon but no other planets – yet.

Fastest spacecraft

NASA's Parker solar probe currently holds the record for the fastest spacecraft ever. It can travel at speeds of up to 176 km every second. That's almost 400 times faster than a fighter jet! It is also the spacecraft to get closest to the Sun and is helping scientists learn about the corona (see pp.24–25).

FAMOUS FIGURE: Dorothy Johnson Vaughan

Dorothy Johnson Vaughan was born in 1910 in the US and played a vital role in the early US space program that allowed people to embark on missions to space. These missions may not have been possible if it weren't for Johnson Vaughan's incredible mathematical skills that helped analyse important data for astronauts.

CREWED SPACECRAFT

Since the 1960s, humans have travelled into space on various spacecraft. They have reached the Moon and the International Space Station. But could they go further? And could space travel become a reality for even more people?

Space shuttles

For many years, space shuttles were a popular way to take astronauts into space. These shuttles were the first reusable spacecrafts. They launched like a rocket but landed like an aeroplane on a runway. The crew could move around inside, within two 'decks' – the flight deck at the top and the mid-deck. Some space shuttles even had laboratories on board for experiments in space.

Back on the ground, people in mission control keep an eye on all aspects of the mission to make sure it goes smoothly.

shuttle to space →

Reusable crafts

Private companies are working to develop modern spacecraft that can be used over and over again. This would reduce the cost of space travel. These spacecraft can take astronauts to the ISS and back, while carrying precious cargo back to Earth too. In the future, could these sorts of spacecraft travel even further, such as to Mars?

Spaceplanes

Scientists are continuously trying to push the limits of space travel. Some companies are exploring technology to create super-powerful engines that could take more people into space. These spaceliners could fly just outside of orbit to travel around the world quicker than aeroplanes, on the edge of space.

FASCINATING FACT

Astronauts eat pre-packaged food that lasts on long journeys and doesn't take up much space. However, scientists have been experimenting with growing fresh food in space – in gardens on the ISS! So far they have grown lettuce, cabbage and other plants.

THE FUTURE OF THE UNIVERSE

Is this the end of your journey through the universe? Is there an end at all? That's a question that top scientists have been asking, and no one knows for sure!

To infinity

It is generally believed that the universe has no defined edge. You couldn't fly to the end and hit a wall. But does it stop? Many scientists believe that ever since it began, the universe has continued to expand. It is probably infinite, with no end at all, or it is very, very big. Either way, there is so much beyond what even the greatest and most powerful telescopes can see.

More questions

The more scientists learn about space, the more they wonder! They now know that there are thousands of planets outside our own solar system, and trillions in our own home galaxy. These great numbers seem promising for life to exist somewhere out there, but so far none has been discovered. Probes continue to travel further and further into deep space in this search for life.

Dark matter

Normal matter makes up everything we can see, including the planets and the stars. Scientists believe this normal matter makes up only about 5 per cent of the universe. Alongside that there is dark energy, as well as dark matter: invisible matter throughout the universe that affects starlight but cannot be detected. This is another area where there are many more questions than answers, and scientists are working hard to discover what this dark matter is made of, and how it works.

Touch down

Even within the known Milky Way galaxy, there are many wonders yet to discover. Space is vast and mysterious, and humans are only beginning to scrape the surface. What will be discovered next?

QUIZ YOURSELF ON...

SPACE EXPLORATION

Are you ready to rocket your learning to the next level? It's time to test your knowledge...

Check your answers on p.89!

1 When did the first artificial satellite launch into space?

A. 1857
B. 1957
C. 1997

2 Who was the first woman in space?

A. Mae Carol Jemison
B. Marie Curie
C. Valentina Tereshkova

The very first telescope was invented by...

A. a spectacle maker
B. a camera maker
C. a mirror maker

Who was the first person to step foot on the Moon?

A. Buzz Aldrin
B. Edwin Hubble
C. Neil Armstrong

TRUE OR FALSE? Travel to the ISS is one thousand times farther than travel to the Moon. **Find out on p.88!**

 Which of the following is not a satellite?

A. the ISS

B. Earth

C. the Sun

 Which planet do rovers explore?

A. Mercury

B. Jupiter

C. Mars

 When did a space probe first land on another planet?

A. 1970

B. 1999

C. 2014

 The fastest spacecraft ever is travelling towards...

A. Venus

B. Pluto

C. the Sun

 Which food has not been grown in space so far?

A. cabbage

B. cocoa beans

C. lettuce

 What is the name of the mysterious invisible matter in the universe?

A. dark matter

B. light matter

C. secret matter

ANSWERS

True or false?

p.17: TRUE. Lyman-alpha Blob 1 is a huge cloud of gas found in the constellation of Aquarius.

p.46: TRUE. Uranus's moons are sometimes known as the 'literary moons' because they're named after some of Shakespeare's most famous characters, like Titania and Oberon from *A Midsummer Night's Dream*.

p.57: TRUE. The Oort Cloud is thought to be incredibly thick!

p.63: FALSE. Unlike on Earth, the daytime sky on Mars is red and the sunset looks blue.

p.87: FALSE. It's the other way around – travel to the Moon is one thousand times farther than travel to the ISS, which is why humans haven't been there as much!

Name that...

pp.20-21: Name that... Constellation

1. Crux (the southern cross)
2. Cygnus (the swan)
3. Scorpius (the scorpion)
4. Gemini (the twins)
5. Canis Major (the great dog)
6. Aquila (the eagle)
7. Orion (the hunter)
8. Lyra (the lyre/harp)

pp.50-51: Name that... Planet

1. Neptune
2. Uranus
3. Jupiter
4. Saturn
5. Earth
6. Mars
7. Mercury
8. Venus

Quiz yourself on...

**pp.62-63: Quiz yourself on...
Objects in space**

1. A. an astronomer
2. B. 13.8 billion years old
3. B. the Milky Way
4. A. main sequence
5. B. 8
6. B. Venus
7. B. Goldilocks Zone
8. A. Human computer
9. C. meteorite
10. C. the Oort Cloud

**pp.86-87: Quiz yourself on...
Space exploration**

1. B. 1957
2. C. Valentina Tereshkova
3. A. a spectacle maker
4. C. Neil Armstrong
5. C. the Sun
6. C. Mars
7. A. 1970
8. C. the Sun
9. B. cocoa beans
10. A. dark matter

GLOSSARY

asterism a small pattern of stars that forms familiar shapes and helps identify areas of the night sky e.g. the Plough

asteroid space rock

asteroid belt a ring of rocky and metallic objects that orbit the Sun – the asteroid belt is located between Mars and Jupiter

astronomer a person that studies space

atmosphere the layer of gases that surrounds Earth

Big Bang the creation of the Universe

black hole very dense clusters of matter packed into a tiny space – the area within the black hole has a strong gravitational pull that nothing can escape, not even light – e.g. Sagittarius A*

Cassini Division the gap between two rings of Saturn

comet a chunk of dirty ice that orbits the Sun – when they get closer to the Sun, they warm up and leave a trail of gas and dust particles

constellation a collection of stars that has been grouped together into a pattern and named after the person, object or creature that is seen in the pattern, e.g. Ursa Major (Great Bear in Latin)

dwarf planet small, nearly round objects in the solar system that are similar to planets but smaller than them

comet

eclipse (lunar) when the Earth gets in the way of the Sun's light hitting the Moon – the Moon usually looks orange for a few hours when this happens

eclipse (solar) when the Sun, Earth and Moon line up and the Moon blocks sunlight from reaching a part of Earth, so it looks like nighttime

exoplanet a planet outside of our solar system, e.g. Kepler-22b

galaxy groups of stars packed together – galaxies come in all different shapes and sizes and can look like spirals, circles, ovals or completely irregular shapes

Goldilocks Zone the area in space not too far from the Sun and not too close to it so that life can exist, i.e. the area where Earth is located

Great Red Spot a giant storm on Jupiter that has been raging for more than 300 years

International Space Station (ISS) a huge space station that orbits Earth – it's like a giant laboratory in space where astronauts carry out research and experiments

Kuiper Belt the doughnut-shaped ring beyond the orbit of Neptune containing icy objects, comets and dwarf planets

light years unit used to measure distances in space

meteor a piece of rock or iron that breaks off an asteroid, is knocked off course and enters Earth's atmosphere

solar eclipse

meteor shower when Earth passes through the debris of a comet or asteroid, a spectacular show of many 'shooting stars' is created. Meteor showers get their name from the constellation that they appear to come from

meteorite a piece of rock or iron that breaks off an asteroid and makes it all the way to Earth's surface

meteoroid a piece of rock or iron that breaks off an asteroid and continues to orbit the Sun

Milky Way spiral galaxy where Earth, the Sun and our solar system is located

the Moon a moon that orbits Earth

nebulae huge clouds of gas and dust which can come from dying stars, and where new stars are born

Olympus Mons the tallest mountain in the solar system, found on Mars

Oort Cloud a zone of icy objects beyond the Kuiper Belt that is thought to surround the entire solar system like a shell

orbit move around

planet a large spherical object (a 3D round object) in space that orbits a star

rocket something that propels and carries another spacecraft into space

rover wheeled robots that land on – and explore – the surface of Mars

satellite an object that orbits a planet or star – satellites can be natural, like the Moon, or artifical (human-made) like satellites that help gather clear photos and data from planets and galaxies

shooting star see meteor shower

solar system the Sun and the group of planets, moons, asteroids and comets that move around it

space probe a research device sent into space without a human pilot

space shuttle a spacecraft that can be used over and over again

space station a spacecraft that stays in orbit for a long period of time

telescope

star balls of gas that give off light and heat

star nursery a nebula where new stars are born

the Sun a yellow dwarf star (formed from a ball of hydrogen and helium gases) – it is the largest and heaviest object in the solar system so its gravity pulls everything else towards it, keeping everything in orbit

supernova when a large star becomes a red supergiant and collapses in a huge explosion

telescope a device that uses mirrors and lenses to make faraway objects look closer

universe all matter and all of space together

white dwarf final stage of a star's life when it cools down and stops shining

INDEX

Aldrin, Edwin 'Buzz' 80
Andromeda Galaxy 13
Armstrong, Neil 65, 80
Arrokoth 54
asterism 19
asteroid 22, 38, 41
asteroid belt 23, 38, 39, 52
astronaut 73–75, 81–83
astronomer 8, 43, 45, 61, 64–66, 68, 69
atmosphere 8
aurora borealis 68, 69
axis 33, 42, 46
Bernardinelli-Bernstein Comet 40
Big Bang 10
Big Dipper (the Plough) 19
black hole 60
booster 64
Callisto 43
capsule 72
Cassini Division 45
Cassini, Giovanni Domenico 45
Ceres 52
Charon 52
comet 22, 40, 41, 55, 56
constellation 18, 19
corona 25–27, 81
crater 28, 34

crewed spacecraft 82, 83
Deimos 36
Dorothy Johnson Vaughan 81
dwarf planet 23, 52, 53
dwarf star 24
Eagle Nebula 17
Earth 32, 33
eclipse 26, 27, 35
eclipse (lunar) 35
eclipse (solar) 26, 27
Edmond Halley 40
Edwin 'Buzz' Aldrin 80
Encke Comet 40
Eris 53, 54
Europa 43
exoplanet 58, 59
flare (solar) 25
Full Moon 34, 35
Gagarin, Yuri 64
galaxy 8, 12
Galilei, Galileo 43, 66
Galileo Galilei 43, 66
Ganymede 43
Gidzenko, Yuri 80
Giovanni Domenico Cassini 45
global positioning system (GPS) 70, 71
Goldilocks Zone 32

GPS (global positioning system) 70, 71
gravitational pull 60
gravity 8, 22, 24
Great Dark Spot 49
Great Red Spot 43
Halley, Edmond 40
Halley's Comet 40
Hans Lippershey 66
Harriot, Thomas 66
Haumea 53, 54
Hawking, Stephen 11
Helix Nebula 16
Hercules 18
ice giant 46–49
inner planet 23
International Space Station (ISS) 65, 73–75, 78, 80, 82, 83
interstellar space 16
Io 43
ISS (International Space Station) 65, 73–75, 78, 80, 82, 83
Jemison, Mae Carol 65
Johnson Vaughan, Dorothy 81
Johnson, Katherine 35
Jupiter 42, 43
Katherine Johnson 35
Kepler-22b 59

Kerss, Tom 68, 69
Krikalev, Sergei 80
Kuiper Belt 23, 53–55
launch tower 73
Leo 18
Leonid meteor shower 19, 41
light year 11
Lippershey, Hans 66
lunar eclipse 35
Mae Carol Jemison 65
main sequence star 14
Makemake 53, 54
Mars 36, 37, 76, 77
Mercury 28, 29
meteor 39
meteor shower 19, 40, 41
meteorite 39
meteoroid 39
Milky Way 12, 17, 58, 61
Moon (the) 26, 34, 35, 66, 78, 80, 82
moons 22, 36, 38, 43–46, 49, 52
mountain 37
nebula 14–17
Neil Armstrong 65, 80
Neptune 48, 49
New Moon 34, 35
Northern Lights 68, 69
observatory 66
ocean 33, 59
Olympus Mons 37
Oort Cloud 23, 56, 57
outer planet 23
Payne-Scott, Ruby 61
Peake, Tim 73
penumbra 35
period of totality 26
Perseid meteor shower 41

phases of the Moon 34, 35
Phobos 36
Pillars of Creation 17
planet 9, 22, 23, 58, 59
Plough (Big Dipper) 19
Pluto 52, 53
Polyakov, Valeri 81
probe 78–81, 85
Proxima Centauri b 58
radiation 61
radio telescope 66
radio wave 61, 64, 66
red giant 15
red planet 36, 37, 76, 77
rocket 64, 72, 73, 81
rocket tower 73
rover 36, 76, 77
Ruby Payne-Scott 61
satellite 70–72
Saturn 44, 45, 79
season 33, 36, 49
Sergei Krikalev 80
Shepherd, William 80
shooting star 19, 39
solar burst 61
solar eclipse 26, 27
solar flare 25
solar storm 61
solar system 22–57
space debris 75
space mission 80, 81
space probe 78–81, 85
space shuttle 64, 82
space station 65
space travel 64, 65
spacecraft 72, 82, 83
spacecraft (crewed) 82, 83
spaceliner 83

spacesuit 75
spacewalk 73, 75
spaghettification 60
star 8, 14, 15, 18, 19, 59, 60
star (main sequence) 14
star nursery 16
static 68, 69
stellar nursery 16
Stephen Hawking 11
Sun 9, 22, 24–30, 40–43, 54–57, 61, 68–71
sunspot 25
supernova 15, 17, 60
telescope 17, 66, 67
telescope (radio) 66
Tereshkova, Valentina 64
Thomas Harriot 66
Tim Peake 73
Titan 44
Tom Kerss 68, 69
toxic 31
Triton 49
umbra 35
universe 10, 11
Uranus 46, 47
Ursa Major (Great Bear) 19
Valentina Tereshkova 64
Valeri Polyakov 81
Venus 30, 31
white dwarf 15
William Shepherd 80
Yuri Gagarin 64
Yuri Gidzenko 80